HARRY STYLES

HEARST
HOME

CONTENTS

WHY
HARRY?
WHY
NOW?

MY NIGHT ON THE TILES
WITH THE REAL PRINCE HARRY

ALEX BILMES
Editor-in-Chief, *Esquire UK*

PAGES 6-7 In April 2022, Harry headlines the opening night of the Coachella Valley Music and Arts Festival wearing a custom multicolored sequin jumpsuit by Gucci. The outfit, with its plunging neckline and flared pants, draws comparisons to the jumpsuit Harry wears in his "As It Was" video.

God knows I've tried to resist Harry Styles, the dinky boyband poppet turned globe-straddling classic rock pasticheur. Not that I haven't admired the hair. We can all agree on the hair. It's so gorgeous, and glossy, and just . . . yum. And the 'fits. Gotta love the 'fits. Not since, ooh, Jagger-Bowie-Prince-insert-name-of-preferred-gender-bending-pop-ledge has anyone had so much fun with a pot of neon nail polish, a feather boa, and a small girl's blouse. The sexy, but not too sexy, videos; the toothsome chat show appearances; the commanding red carpet sashays: Anyone can see the guy is a pro. No wonder he has so totally eclipsed his former bandmates in One Direction, none of whose names many of us can remember. Nick? Simon? Ronan? Jason? Abs? Ginger? Am I getting warmer?

Harry Styles is the pop star of the moment, and there's no point arguing with it. If the overall effect is less lock-up-your-daughters than take-him-home-to-mum, then perhaps that's what makes Styles the perfect chart-topper for our turbulent times. He's charming, he's clean cut, he has beautiful manners (and great hair!), and he's as progressive as you like.

This is, indisputably, not the moment for a straight white male pop god manque to project the old rock 'n' roll values of edge, danger, sexual voraciousness, and questionable lifestyle choices. And Harry doesn't. He does cute; he does soft; he does sugary; he does palatable. He's an Aperol spritz, just the one, in the guise of a long line of coke.

The whole world might be going to hell, but at least we've got Harry to wrap us in his warm embrace and then cook us a macrobiotic breakfast in the morning while asking tenderly after our mental health. "Late Night Talking" is the title of one of his songs. Late night *talking*? I mean, jeez, how very *sweet*.

Like so many of us, Styles is in thrall to the soothing sounds and foppish styles of singer-songwritin' 1970s Los Angeles, especially imperial phase Fleetwood Mac. Also yacht-rock earworms of the Steely Dan, 10CC variety. On the *Harry's House* album, you can hear all of that, plus less feted outfits of my own youth. Johnny Hates Jazz comes to mind, possibly for the first time since 1987.

Obliging to a fault, Styles does the pop critics' work for them: the first track on *Harry's House* was called "Music

HE'S AN APEROL SPRITZ, JUST THE ONE, IN THE GUISE OF A LONG LINE OF COKE. 💜

for a Sushi Restaurant," which nicely sums up his brand of pleasantly nonconfrontational background noodling. He got it in there first, even though "getting it in there first" is the last thing you could typically say about Harry Styles, so determinedly retro is his approach.

He has impeccable taste, then. If you went to Harry's actual house—in Laurel Canyon *of course*—no doubt you'd find *Nilsson Schmilsson* playing on the vintage turntable, an original Barney Bubbles on the wall, and a wardrobe full of Nudie suits like those Gram Parsons used to wear, and a glass of cloudy orange wine waiting for you on the deck, where Harry is just finishing up a Pilates class.

What does it all add up to? Not much and, in the contemporary fashion-speak, everything. *Harry's House* breaks absolutely no new ground in any shape or form. It was a warm bath to wash your cares away, with candles and a chamomile tea. And who'd say no to that right now?

Incidentally, but perhaps instructively, I have my own brief Harry Styles encounter to share. A few years ago, prepandemic, I attended a fabulous party in Rome, at an ancient museum on a hill. There was a dazzling catwalk show and then endless champagne in a beautiful garden and, at some point, rumors began to circulate about a secret late-night performance by no less a superstar than Stevie Nicks. The hour grew late and the crowd began to thin, but a few of us dipsomaniacal hopefuls stayed on, FOMO trumping hopes of a few hours' kip before the early flight home. And then, sure enough, for an audience of not more than 200, Fleetwood Mac's original witchy gypsy fire woman and her band—Waddy Wachtel on guitar!—took to a tiny stage and began to play the hits: "Rhiannon," "Gypsy," "Edge of Seventeen." "Oh my God," swooned my pal Jerry, hand on chest failing to still his beating heart as he slipped into fashion-French: *"Je* die!"

Stevie was everything you'd hope for: funny, delicate, mesmerizing. And then Harry Styles shuffled to the side of the stage, and the band struck up the opening chords to the sublime "Landslide," and I thought, quite frankly, do us a favor, Styles. You may be a dandy heartbreaker of considerable starry charisma, but we are in the presence of classic rock royalty. Know your limitations.

Then he began to sing, in duet with Stevie, and the place went completely guano. The boy can really hold a note, and he has stadium-size presence, and suddenly it was possible to see what all the fuss is about. To a man, woman, and nongendered person, we were all utterly smitten. We climbed that mountain, and we turned around. And yes— how could it be otherwise?—the landslide brought us down.

Later still, in the wee small hours, a handful of us, including me, Jerry, and Harry Styles, piled into a people carrier. We were driven to a nightclub and ushered into a room where shirtless young men threw their well-muscled arms in the air to the insistent thumping of a heavy beat. The noise was deafening, but through a combination of shouting in ears and hand signals, Jerry was able to establish that we would all like something, anything, to drink. He returned from the bar with pints of lager. So hot and sweaty was it on that dancefloor that, during an energetic moment of Diana Ross–induced bodyslamming, someone (not a member of our group) dropped his pint. The glass shattered into pieces. Being the selfless, community-spirited people that we are, we ignored this and carried on throwing shapes.

Not Harry. Unseen, I believe, by anyone but me, he picked up an empty glass from the bar and, in his magical, jewel-encrusted, flared Gucci suit, crouched down on the floor and painstakingly retrieved each piece of jagged-edged glass from under the heels of the revelers who continued to cavort around him, unaware that a handsome A-lister was kneeling at their dancing feet, trying to save them from a nasty cut.

It's a small thing, no doubt, the sort of behavior any of us would like to think we'd exhibit under the circumstances. (Although I, for one, hadn't bothered, preferring to keep my own, less heavily embellished suit stain-free and my fingers safe from being stepped on.) But it struck me as representative of the boy's appeal. What a nice, thoughtful, well-brought-up young man, I thought. OK, so he's no Lou Reed. But maybe that's OK. Maybe Lou Reed isn't who we need right now.

The tit tattoos? They're just a bonus.

Harry introduces Stevie at the 2019 Rock & Roll Hall of Fame inductions at the Barclays Center in New York City. He refers to her as "the magical gypsy godmother who occupies the in between," who he admires for being herself, and "by being so unapologetically herself, she gives others permission to do the same." The Rock & Roll Hall of Fame adds this suit to its permanent Right Here, Right Now exhibit shortly after the ceremony.

THE SOUND

CALCULATED
RISKS

JEM ASWAD
Senior Music Editor, *Variety*

PAGES 14-15
Harry—wearing a custom white silk bell-bottom Gucci suit—waves to fans at a show at Madison Square Garden in New York on June 21, 2018.

After billions of dollars in ticket sales, countless billions of streams, and multiplatinum album sales in nearly every major country across the globe, the success of Harry Styles's solo career sometimes appears effortless and inevitable. Granted, as the boy-most-likely-to from One Direction, the mega popular pop group of their era, Harry did have a seemingly surefire launching pad: All he had to do was more of the same. But he hasn't done that. Instead, he's taken calculated musical risks that were much more daring than they might seem, and they've paid off so beautifully.

The leap from teen star to career artist is a challenging one that few can pull off. Leaving the nest of a successful group, especially one that started when the members were teenagers, is one of the most difficult challenges an artist can face: Now that you're on your own, free of the group and the machine around it, what are you going to be? Many have tried and come up short.

Harry launched his solo career with a self-titled album in May 2017 (around 18 months after 1D played its final concert), and it sounded like nothing else in the market at the time. Indeed, with its 1970s sonic references, *Harry Styles* sounded like nothing that had been released in decades. The first single was not a Justin Timberlake–sized banger. Instead "Sign of the Times," a slow, string-drenched, swooning ballad, is reminiscent of Harry Nilsson's 1972 smash "Without You," while other songs recall Elton John and Fleetwood Mac. And the most single-seeming song on the album, "Two Ghosts," sounds more like a country jam than a pop hit.

Yet for all its genre- and generation-spanning success— *Harry Styles*'s retro sound spoke to not only his audience but their parents as well. It succeeded in its main goal: cleaning the palate as a musical reboot that would allow Styles to go anywhere he wanted afterward.

Which, with *Fine Line* in 2019, was the combination of the organic feel of his debut and the direction everyone had expected him to go in the first place—a sort of effervescent contemporary pop with roots in classic analog sounds. (Styles cited solo Paul McCartney as a key influence on this one.) But the differentiator between *Fine Line* and his debut is the blissful pop rush of the songs, which would form the bulk of his set lists on his coming tours: "Watermelon Sugar," "Cherry," "Treat People With Kindness," "Adore You," and other tunes that, once you've seen them performed, will forever summon the vision of Styles running across an arena stage, arms outstretched, taking in and giving back the love from the crowd.

"I JUST TRY AND MAKE STUFF THAT I LIKE AND THAT I THINK SOUNDS COOL AND SOUNDS GOOD... YOU CAN'T REALLY ENGINEER PEOPLE LIKING MUSIC TOO MUCH, AND I ACTUALLY THINK THAT'S FREEING."

**—HARRY DISCUSSING *HARRY'S HOUSE*
ON Z100 NEW YORK ON APRIL 1, 2022**

However, it would be some time before he would get back on stage. *Fine Line* was released in December 2019 and the tour was set to start in April 2020. Then COVID-19 brought the world to a standstill and the first show wouldn't open until September 2021. Since then, Harry hasn't really stopped. Whereas most artists release an album and then tour behind it, Styles spent the pandemic working on his third album, *Harry's House*; played a major world tour; then paused for just a dozen-odd weeks before launching what was basically part two of Love on Tour, this one incorporating the more introspective songs from *Harry's House* while still having *Fine Line* as its baseline.

With "As It Was," a blockbuster lead single and arguably the biggest hit of 2022, *Harry's House* could have been filled out with piano ballads and still been a pop smash. (In fact, the album earned him two Grammy Awards.) Yet the introspection of this album extended to the lyrics as well. Styles has a rare ability to make big statements in few words. For example, the lyrics to "Treat People With Kindness" don't really say much, but when he's singing the song onstage while waving a rainbow flag—or wearing gender-norm-breaking clothes, or helping fans come out at his concerts, or making brief statements like "We're all a little bit gay"—it says everything.

Six years into his solo career, Harry Styles has proved that the path from boy-band stardom to a lasting solo career doesn't have to be a safe or obvious one—that an artist can take risks with their music and profile and see those risks pay off. For Harry, they've paid off in artistic and commercial ways, but he's also become a leader and a champion of causes he believes in, perhaps most of all because he respects the intelligence and open-mindedness of his fans, who probably feel that they've been walking alongside him—never following—every step of the way.

Harry poses with his Best Pop Vocal Album and Album of the Year Grammy awards on February 5, 2023.

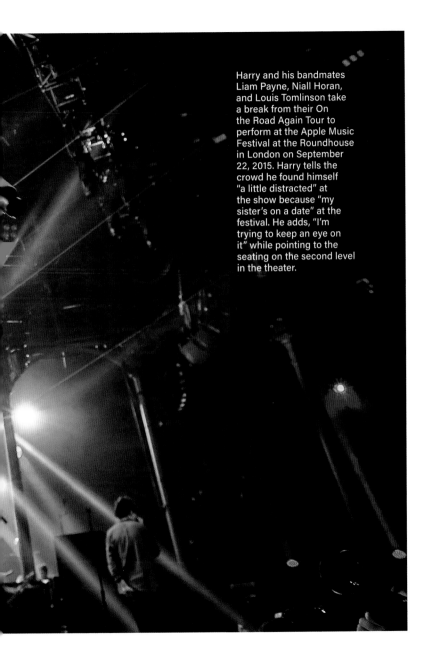

Harry and his bandmates Liam Payne, Niall Horan, and Louis Tomlinson take a break from their On the Road Again Tour to perform at the Apple Music Festival at the Roundhouse in London on September 22, 2015. Harry tells the crowd he found himself "a little distracted" at the show because "my sister's on a date" at the festival. He adds, "I'm trying to keep an eye on it" while pointing to the seating on the second level in the theater.

LEFT Harry poses with Mick Jagger, a favorite singer of his since childhood, at the Fonda Theatre in Los Angeles in 2015. The One Direction alum has been likened to a modern-day Mick, and the Rolling Stones singer admitted to *The Press*, "I can see the influence."

RIGHT After One Direction's indefinite hiatus began in January 2016, fans wondered whether Harry would release solo music. In April 2017, he finally confirms a debut album. Harry had escaped to Jamaica to compose the rock-heavy set, with the intent of making "an album that I wanted to listen to," he tells *The New York Times*. The album art shows Harry's naked back as he partially submerges himself in a pink bath, offering a peek at his tattoos.

Harry, in a Charles Jeffrey double-breasted jumpsuit, serves attitude while performing "Kiwi" during his four-night residency on *The Late Late Show With James Corden* in May 2017. Stylers speculate that "Kiwi" is about one of his exes, but as always, Harry keeps it vague, telling BBC Radio 1 only that the tune "started out as a joke," but "now it's one of my favorite songs."

Harry performed twice with One Direction on *Saturday Night Live*, then came back as a solo artist on April 15, 2017, to belt out "Sign of the Times" in a double-breasted, wide-lapel plaid Gucci suit from Alessandro Michele's fall 2017 collection. He abandons the jacket when he returns later in the evening to premiere "Ever Since New York."

On May 15, 2017, days after the release of his self-titled debut solo album, Harry prepares to kick off his weeklong residency at *The Late Late Show With James Corden* in an embroidered Gucci suit. Later on Instagram, the show posts that Harry "melted everyone's faces" with his "searing rendition" of "Sign of the Times."

Though Harry has always kept it vague when commenting on his sexuality, the star consistently supports the LGBTQ community. When kicking off Live on Tour in San Francisco on September 19, 2017—his first tour date as a solo artist—Harry displays a pride flag on his microphone stand and dances with it after an audience member tosses it up to him. Later, during Love on Tour, Harry helps an audience member come out to their family.

RIGHT With just a microphone and his guitar, Harry gives the chilling debut performance of "Two Ghosts" in a Burberry tunic shirt with a ruffled collar and cuffs on *The Late Late Show With James Corden* on May 17, 2017. In a sketch that also airs that night, Harry and pal James prove how their love of singing can sometimes be inappropriate, as they burst into song while performing surgery and defusing a bomb.

PAGES 32–33 Harry douses the adoring crowd with water at the Greek Theatre in Los Angeles on September 20, 2017. For the occasion, he sports a custom turquoise-and-gold Gucci suit, a black shirt, and a pussy bow. "Thank you for coming to see me when I've only got 10 songs," he tells the crowd during the 80-minute set.

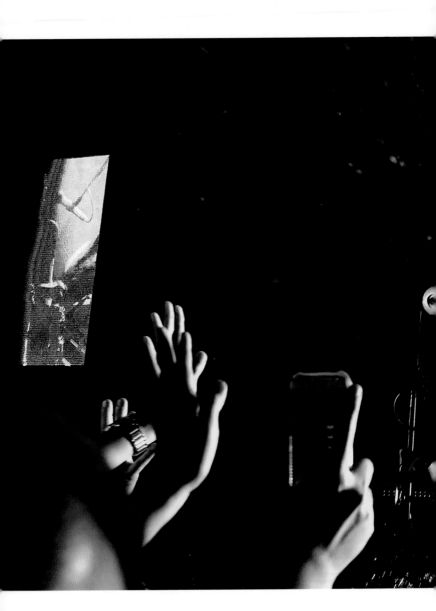

Harry, in a custom black double-breasted Gucci suit, a bubblegum pink silk shirt, and Gucci horse-bit ankle boots, opens the Victoria's Secret Fashion Show on November 20, 2017, in Shanghai, China, with his deep-rock cut "Kiwi." The event proves to be somewhat of a reunion of exes for Harry, with models Nadine Leopold, Sara Sampaio, and Georgia Fowler all walking in the show.

Harry dresses to match the red interior of Radio City Music Hall when he performs in September 2017. Fittingly, he opens with "Ever Since New York." Harry sports a one-of-a-kind metallic red-and-black floral silk jacquard Gucci suit worn over a black silk shirt with a self-tie collar. "Hello, New York. My name is Harry. I'm from England," he sweetly tells the crowd.

Harry grooves in a custom Alexander McQueen paisley suit, wide-leg trousers, and a cream silk crepe de chine shirt while performing "Kiwi" at the 31st Annual Australian Recording Industry Association Music Awards in Sydney on November 28, 2017. Later, as he accepts the best international artist award, Harry celebrates the country's recent decision to legalize same-sex marriage. "Everyone here has always been so wonderful to me," Harry says. "Thank you so much for having me and having me back, and congratulations on your recent political decision."

Harry wears a custom white silk bell-bottom Gucci suit stitched with black floral embroidery over a black pussy-bow blouse during his Live on Tour Madison Square Garden performance in June 2018. The phrases *memento mori* (Latin for "remember your mortality") and *jardin d'hiver* (French for "winter garden," possibly in reference to the name of the concert venue) appear embroidered next to select blooms.

LEFT Harry shares his second album, *Fine Line*, with a group of his biggest fans at a Spotify Listening Party in Los Angeles on December 11, 2019. The event transports attendees to the fictional land of Eroda, complete with imaginary locations like Harry's Little Blue Bedroom and the Fisherman's Pub, where the singer appears onstage in a Babar-print Lanvin graphic knitted cardigan. *Fine Line* gives Harry his second number one solo album.

RIGHT On the cover of his sophomore album, Harry appears in another custom Gucci outfit: a magenta button-down shirt with matching suspenders and high-waist, wide-leg white pants. It joins the ranks of Harry's most iconic ensembles. *Fine Line* tackles heartbreak, infidelity, and rocky relationships and scores Harry the largest sales week for an album by a solo U.K. male artist since Nielsen started keeping track in 1991.

RIGHT AND PAGES 44-45 In a lilac chiffon Gucci dress plus flared brown pants, Harry submerges himself underwater in the music video for "Falling." Harry tells New Zealand radio DJ Zane Lowe that he wrote the song in "a big moment where I was asking myself, 'Who am I? What am I doing?'"

ABOVE Lizzo stuns the crowd at her Super Bowl LIV weekend concert in Miami on January 30, 2020, by bringing out Harry to duet on her hit "Juice." Harry dons a cropped sweater vest over a button-down shirt that he pairs with bell-bottom pants for the surprise appearance.

LEFT Harry plays host and serves as musical guest on *The Late Late Show With James Corden* on December 10, 2019. For his performance of "Adore You," the rocker chooses a Gucci polka-dot suit and jazzes it up even more with a silk yellow necktie and his signature statement rings. Harry wrote "Adore You" in just one day and tells Entercom, "It's about that initial infatuation stage when you get that heavy feeling of just bliss, like a blissful, very joyous connection with someone."

Harry chooses a light blue mohair intarsia crewneck sweater by Gucci for his March 2020 appearance on NPR's *Tiny Desk Concert*. "It just feels like you're in the way," he jokes of performing in the cramped Washington, DC, office. He eventually settles in and sings "Watermelon Sugar," revealing that Richard Brautigan's book *In Watermelon Sugar* inspired him.

On May 18, 2020, Harry drops the music video for "Watermelon Sugar" and fills it with fun fashion and cheeky double entendres. Harry mixes Gucci items, vintage '70s looks, and bold, bright prints to convey the track's sexy sentiments that make it that summer's anthem. From his signature pearls and a skinny scarf to a smattering of knitwear and retro sunglasses, the video, which filmed on the same Malibu beach as 1D's "What Makes You Beautiful," shows off Harry's penchant for whimsical, statement-making styles. The strategic fruit placement and Harry's animated facial expressions nod to the fact that the song playfully details the female orgasm.

LEFT Shirtless and leather-clad, Harry opens the 63rd Annual Grammy Awards in Los Angeles in March 2021 with "Watermelon Sugar." The song wins Harry his first Grammy, for best pop solo performance. "I think people could assume that, as he was performing his single 'Watermelon Sugar,' his look would reflect the music video," Harry's stylist Harry Lambert tells *British Vogue*. "We wanted to twist that on its head and go for something darker, sexier, and more unexpected."

PAGE 54 Made of faux fur, the green boa that Harry ditches before indulging in a dance break at the March 2021 Grammys is one of three he wears that night—beginning the evening in a purple Gucci feather boa and ending it in a black one. Per global shopping app Lyst, page views for feather boas see a 1,500% spike in the 48 hours following the awards show. Lambert "wanted to do something that felt British and eccentric."

PAGE 55 During his performance, Harry's chest tattoos—a butterfly and two swallows—are on full display. "I like that kind of style of tattoos, like the old sailor kind of tattoos," Harry told *Us Weekly* in 2012 about the two songbirds on his pecs. "They symbolize traveling, and we [in One Direction] travel a lot!" The butterfly, which he got inked in 2013, symbolized an early transformation for Styles but he has not discussed its exact meaning.

Harry embraces dainty touches in the "Golden" music video, such as the delicate beaded Éliou necklace that spells out *golden*. He filmed the video for the ethereal indie pop track in Maiori, on the Amalfi Coast of Italy, specifically on the town's Path of Lemons and the Valle dei Mulini hike. "It's like driving down the coast—that's what the song is for," Harry says of the chill tune, which won Global Hit of the Year at the MTV Millennial Awards in 2021.

After being delayed by the COVID-19 pandemic, Love on Tour kicks off at MGM Grand Garden Arena in Las Vegas on September 4, 2021. For the occasion, Harry sports an all-red Gucci outfit featuring a glittery fringe vest and high-waisted trousers. "Vegas, you blew me away. I'd been waiting for that," Harry tweets after the show. Throughout the tour, fans show up in Harry-inspired looks, rocking boas, flared pants, and '70s fashions.

Harry packs his "As It Was" video, which he shot over two days in London in February 2022 with Ukrainian director Tanu Muino, with multiple high-end fashion moments. He starts out in a long red coat by menswear designer Bianca Saunders, a fuzzy black Dries Van Noten scarf, and leather gloves before unveiling a custom red sequined jumpsuit by Arturo Obegero. Fans love the look—so much so that the search for "men's jumpsuits" jumps 212% after the March 2022 release of the video. The catchy synth-pop first single from his third album breaks the record for Spotify's most streamed track in 24 hours by a male artist.

LEFT Harry turns things upside down on the cover of *Harry's House*. He strays from Gucci and ushers in an age of delicate fashion in an outfit from Molly Goddard's Spring 2022 collection. Written during the COVID-19 pandemic, *Harry's House*, like his past two solo albums, debuts at number one. It is also the fastest-selling album in the United Kingdom in 2022, and it gives Harry the rare honor of having the top album and song ("As It Was") in 11 countries, including the U.K. and the U.S.

RIGHT One week after releasing *Harry's House*, the superstar headlines BBC Radio 1's Big Weekend festival at War Memorial Park in Coventry, England. Harry wears a custom Arturo Obegero sequined jumpsuit.

Harry selects a classic Canadian tuxedo to rehearse—in the rain!—for his *Today* show concert at Rockefeller Plaza in New York City in May 2022. The custom shearling-collar denim jacket and jeans from AMI Paris draw inspiration from the label's fall 2022 collection.

After nearly three years without new music, Harry releases *Harry's House* on May 20, 2022. The day before the highly anticipated record drops, Harry electrifies the morning—and cements *Harry's House* as the start of his jumpsuit phase—in a candy-striped neon-yellow, brown, and black one-piece by JW Anderson on the *Today* show. The pattern pulls from a dress in Anderson's resort 2022 collection. "It's early, so I wanted to be comfortable," Harry explains to *Today* host Hoda Kotb. "I thought, Sleeping bag, babygro [sleepsuit]—I'm going for comfort."

Harry loves to load up on rings. He accents his *Today* show jumpsuit with a vintage 14-karat yellow gold one featuring a cultured pearl and diamond flower from Sophie Jane Jewels and the Gucci *H* and *S* initials. In an interview during the show, Harry reveals that he had lost his beloved Gucci lion ring after performing at Coachella but got it back the day before thanks to a fan who tracked it down.

Harry enlists James Corden to film the music video for "Daylight" on a tight $300 budget over three hours in a Brooklyn apartment. The duo knock on random doors around the neighborhood and then find a group of four fans willing to let Harry shoot the video in their home for *The Late Late Show With James Corden*. "I cannot stress enough that this was James's idea," Harry quips.

Harry slays in a retro bespoke Palomo Spain jumpsuit and classic
black Vans at Capital's Summertime Ball at Wembley Stadium
in London on June 12, 2022. A similar look appears in the label's
Spring 2022 runway show, but Harry's version lacks the
brand's logo and adds a black belt. While singing "Late Night
Talking" Harry catches a rainbow flag thrown to him by a fan.

Harry morphs into a bearded merman for the "Music for a Sushi Restaurant" music video, released in October 2022. Harry tells NPR that the idea for the song title came when he heard a song from *Fine Line* playing at a sushi restaurant in Los Angeles. "I was like, 'This is really strange music for a sushi restaurant,'" he explains. "And then I was like, "Oh, that would be a really fun…title.""

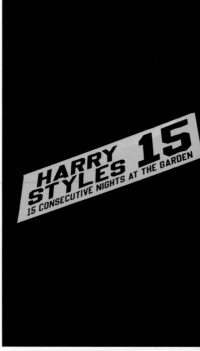

HARRY STYLES 15
15 CONSECUTIVE NIGHTS AT THE GARDEN

From August 20 to September 21, 2022, Harry takes up residency at Madison Square Garden in New York City for 10 sold-out shows and then adds 5 more to meet demand. Harry wears a range of statement pieces, including this striped sequin set with tank with a deep V-neck on the final night of the run. Before the show's encore, *CBS Mornings* cohost Gayle King honors Harry with a banner commemorating his 15 consecutive sold-out shows, saying, "No artist has ever done that before." Harry becomes one of three musical artists with an MSG flag, joining Billy Joel and Phish.

Harry celebrates his 29th birthday on February 1, 2023, with a concert in Palm Springs, California, the last U.S. stop on his Love on Tour. Dressed in a two-tone pink custom Gucci rhinestone jacket and pants set for the occasion, Harry told the 11,000-person crowd, "Obviously, I have a fear of people not coming to my birthday party. So I just thought I would do a show and maybe you might come." No birthday party would be complete without serenading the guest of honor with "Harry Birthday," so the concertgoers do just that. He also blows out candles on a cake during the show and rocks a floppy birthday hat.

LEFT Nominated in six categories at the 65th Annual Grammy Awards on February 5, 2023, *Harry's House* wins two catagories—Best Pop Vocal Album and Album of the Year. Other nominees for the latter were Adele, Beyoncé, and Lizzo.

ABOVE LEFT Actor Stanley Tucci and Harry strike up an unexpected bromance, embracing when Stanley presents Harry with the Album of the Year award for *Harry's House* at the 2023 BRIT Awards. "There's literally no one I love more in the world than Stanley Tucci, so this means so much," Harry tells the audience.

ABOVE RIGHT Harry wins all four BRIT Award categories in which he was nominated: Song of the Year, Album of the Year, Artist of the Year, and Best Pop/R&B Act. "I'm really, really grateful for this, and I'm very aware for my privilege up here tonight, so this award is for Rina, Charli, Florence, Mabel, and Becky," he says while accepting the Best Pop/R&B Act award, citing his fellow nominees.

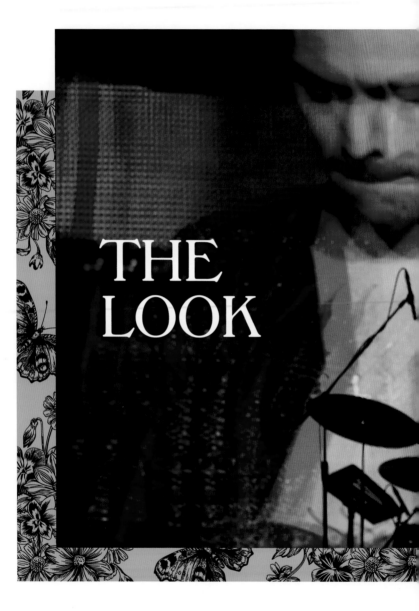

THE
LOOK

FASHION
FLUENCY

AYA KANAI
Head of Creative and Editorial, Google Shopping

Harry's successful music career proves he knows how to make a splash, and he did that again when he became the first man ever to appear solo on the cover of U.S. *Vogue*. Dressed in a frothy, lace-trimmed periwinkle Gucci gown and black double-breasted tuxedo jacket, he shocked many critics and delighted others, making a statement about gender stereotypes and provoking an important conversation about tolerance, creativity, and freedom of expression.

Harry's personal style is his essential creative medium, second only to his music, and it has redefined notions of masculinity to include traditionally feminine flourishes. Slick layouts for fashion magazines find him wearing boundary-pushing looks, including a Comme des Garçons Homme Plus blazer and kilt set, a Victorian crinoline by

Harris Reed, and a suit with 1980s shoulders and zoot-suit wide leg pants, softly draped. He embraces sequins, lace pussy bow blouses, feather boas, and color-block-knitted cardigans and all the bold colors of the rainbow in his everyday wardrobe. He often accessorizes with his chunky signature rings, nail polish in many colors, pearl necklaces, oversize glasses, and those famous tattoos.

As is often the case in fashion and culture, today's controversy becomes tomorrow's norm. Menswear collections now include skirts—both tailored and flouncy—floral and pastel blouses, and knitted or fuzzy cardigans, not to mention the tattoos and jewelry sported by androgynous models stalking the catwalk. Every wardrobe move Harry makes is emulated by fashion fans and eagerly studied and stocked by fashion retailers worldwide. Harry has been very good for both the business of fashion and the business of self-expression.

Another thing is for sure: Harry is a skillful storyteller. Pop stars used to maintain an elusive distance from their fans. Now, most people hold a communication tool in the palm of their hands, with a direct line to the mega-famous. But Harry manages to strike a balance between mystery and accessibility, giving his audience just enough to feel like they have a sense of him and yet not enough to really know him. He dances with his fans on all social platforms, as only

"I'LL PUT ON SOMETHING THAT FEELS REALLY FAMBOYANT....I THINK IF YOU GET SOMETHING YOU FEEL AMAZING IN, IT'S LIKE A SUPERHERO OUTFIT."

—HARRY ON HIS U.S. *VOGUE* COVER SHOOT, DECEMBER 2022

a canny professional could. Fans post videos of his every move in concert and, of course, of every new performance outfit. And they've adopted his signature boa as their own, sporting them proudly around town.

If fashion is a language, Harry speaks it fluently. Although musicians before him like David Bowie and Prince broke gender norms with personal style, their brazen approach was intended to shock and was part of a revolutionary rallying cry for their generations. Harry is simply Harry; he comes across as happy and at ease in his own skin and fashion choices. But in the new world of viral trends on social media platforms, Harry's effect permeates pop culture in deep, far-reaching, and immediate ways, most noticeably among the younger generation of his fans. Gen Z fashion questions previously held standards and expectations— from the way clashing colors, patterns, and textures are worn together in new and exciting ways (and also in a throwback to '70s style) to a shattering of the now seemingly old-fashioned male-female dichotomy. Harry nods to those trends through his outfit choices and reveals a strategic understanding of the psyche of his young fan base. His style is genius in that it's gorgeous, political, tolerant, and loving, and it's shrewdly woven into his overarching creative point of view. His fashion, like his songs, takes center stage.

Harry makes history as the first solo man on the cover of *Vogue* in December 2020. Inside, he appears in more gender-fluid looks, like a blazer and kilt by Comme des Garçons Homme Plus, Falke socks, and brogues.

In April 2012, Harry and One Direction take their Up All Night Tour international for the first time with a stop in Sydney. Crowds of screaming fans pack Hordern Pavilion to see the boys, who wear the complementary outfits that mark a boy band's unifying look. They play songs from their debut album; a medley of hits, including Black Eyed Peas' "I Gotta Feeling," Gym Class Heroes' "Stereo Hearts," and Ednaswap's "Torn"; and a cover of Kings of Leon's "Use Somebody.

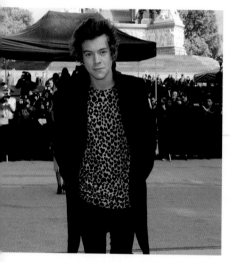

LEFT Harry shows his spots at the Burberry Prorsum womenswear Spring/Summer 2014 show during London Fashion Week in September 2013. He later put the animal-print shirt up for auction and donated the $4,845.53 proceeds from the sale to UNICEF.

RIGHT While still with One Direction, Harry begins to show off his eclectic style at the 2015 American Music Awards with this black-and-white floral suit from Gucci's Spring/Summer 2016 menswear collection. Harry's 2018 *jardin d'hiver* suit (page 38) echoes this one. This marks the beginning of Harry's collaboration with Gucci and creative director Alessandro Michele, who joined the Italian fashion house in January 2015. Alessandro announced his departure from Gucci in November 2022.

Harry appears on *The Graham Norton Show* in April 2017 and opts for a custom black Gucci suit with velvet-trimmed collar and lapels. The flared trousers are embroidered with silk dragons. Comedian Rob Brydon, who appears with Harry on the episode, jokes after the performance, "You got the pajamas I sent you, I see."

For his *Today* show concert in New York City on May 9, 2017—his second live solo performance—Harry embraces millennial pink with an Edward Sexton suit. He sings "Ever Since New York," "Carolina," and "Sign of the Times." During Harry's interview with Hoda Kotb, he greets a family that had driven 11 hours from Michigan to attend the show.

At the 2017 Victoria's Secret Fashion Show in Shanghai, Harry tones it down to keep the spotlight on the Angels. After opening the show in a pink and black Gucci outfit (see page 34), he changes into a Givenchy mint wool and mohair suit and matching shirt reminiscent of the 1970s.

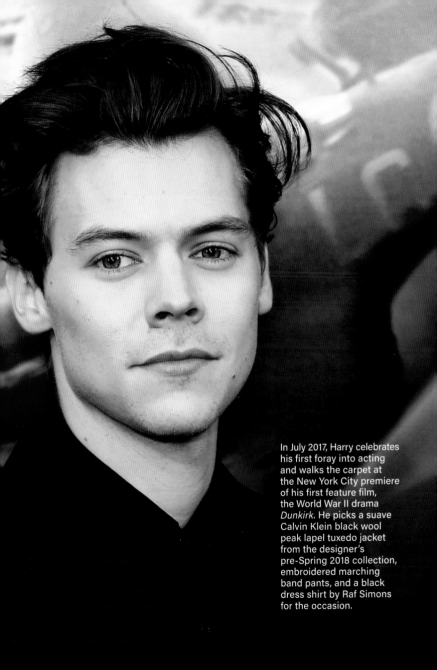

In July 2017, Harry celebrates his first foray into acting and walks the carpet at the New York City premiere of his first feature film, the World War II drama *Dunkirk*. He picks a suave Calvin Klein black wool peak lapel tuxedo jacket from the designer's pre-Spring 2018 collection, embroidered marching band pants, and a black dress shirt by Raf Simons for the occasion.

On day one of the 2017 iHeartMusic Festival in Las Vegas, Harry tumbles down the rabbit hole and performs his five-song set in a custom Gucci velvet suit reminiscent of the Queen of Hearts from *Alice in Wonderland*. When Harry unbuttons his jacket, he reveals a semisheer, patterned white shirt.

Harry firmly establishes his solo debut period as one of whimsical suits when he shows up to the BBC Radio studios in London in a red bespoke Vivienne Westwood checked suit and stacked-heel Gucci snaffle loafers on May 12, 2017, to promote his album *Harry Styles*.

For a May 27, 2017, performance, Harry slips into a Gucci two-button notch-lapel brown mohair suit with blue, orange, and red embroidered dragon details running down the pant leg and curling over the shoulder.

LEFT Harry hits a home run with this homage to Elton John at the Casamigos Halloween party in Las Vegas in 2018. The uniform and oversize glasses are like the ones the "Rocket Man" singer wore to play Dodger Stadium in Los Angeles in 1975.

RIGHT While in New York City to rehearse for *Saturday Night Live* in November 2019, Harry rocks a quirky sheep-printed wool sweater vest by Lanvin, part of the French fashion house's Spring/Summer 2020 collection. Fans wondered whether Harry drew inspiration from Princess Diana, who wore a red sweater covered in sheep to a polo match in 1983.

Harry and Gucci creative director Alessandro Michele walk the pink carpet at the 2019 Met Gala, for which they served as cochairs. The theme is camp. Harry's stylist, Harry Lambert, described the look to *Vogue* as "taking traditionally feminine elements like the frills, heeled boots, sheer fabric, and the pearl earring, but then rephrasing them as masculine pieces."

As the *Saturday Night Live* host on November 16, 2019, Harry wears a color-blocked getup from Gucci's Spring 2020 menswear show, covering a blue dress shirt with a light gray double-breasted blazer atop yellow wide-leg trousers. Harry concludes his opening monologue behind the piano. His hands never stop playing, even as he sips a martini.

Filling in for his pal as host of *The Late Late Show With James Corden* in December 2019, Harry sports a custom brown Gucci suit with a striped double-breasted jacket, matching waistcoat, and straight-leg trousers. During the show, Harry chats with actress Tracee Ellis Ross and his ex-girlfriend Kendall Jenner, and he even plays a game of Spill Your Guts or Fill Your Guts with the reality TV star, during which they confirm their since-ended relationship for the first time.

ABOVE LEFT For an exclusive concert in New York City hosted by SiriusXM and Pandora in February 2020, Harry pivots to another favorite designer, Lanvin, for this layered, multipatterned look from its fall 2020 menswear collection.

ABOVE RIGHT For a visit to BBC Radio 2 in London on February 14, 2020, Harry keeps up his trend of wearing flared pants and pearl necklaces. He tops corduroy trousers and a striped T-shirt with a Bode green appliquéd wool-twill jacket featuring red and white cross-stitching detail.

ABOVE LEFT In his first of three outfits at the 2020 BRIT Awards, Harry wears a double-breasted chocolate brown suit from Gucci's Fall/Winter 2020 collection, along with a separate lace Peter Pan collar, a pearl necklace, and lavender nail polish.

ABOVE RIGHT Harry stops by SiriusXM's New York City studio on March 2, 2020, wearing a mix of custom and runway Gucci items: a blue crewneck sweater over a penny-collar blouse, lime green wide-leg pleated trousers, and white boots. Harry adds a string of pearls to pull together the casual chic outfit. During the Harry chats with Howard Stern about being inspired by Paul McCartney. "Y want to be the guy who's 70 and playing for three hours because he can wants to and everyone's loving it," Harry says.

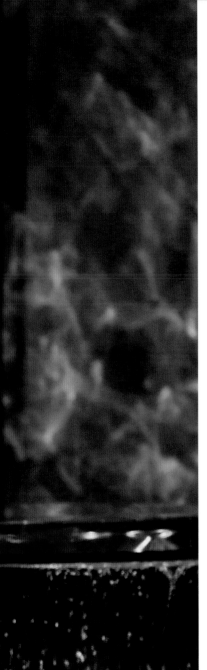

Harry told *Variety* that he doesn't shy away from wearing women's garments because "to not wear [something] because it's females' clothing, you shut out a whole world of great clothes." He makes good on that statement at the 2020 BRIT Awards, when he wears a lace jumpsuit from Marc Jacobs's womenswear line paired with matching gloves to debut his song "Falling."

Harry ends the night at the 2020 BRIT Awards in a bright yellow Marc Jacobs suit from the designer's Spring 2020 collection, plus a lavender polka-dot button-up blouse and matching purple tulle scarf tied in the front and a pin that reads "Treat People With Kindness." (Lady Gaga wore the same look, topped with a hat, on the December 2019 cover of *Elle*.)

PAGES 116-117 Harry gives major '80s aesthetic on the *Today* show on February 26, 2020, in a custom pink double-breasted blazer, eggplant-colored flared trousers, a cheerful polka-dot tie, and white loafers from Gucci's Spring 2020 collection. He brings a fan named Mary to tears by presenting her with tickets to his upcoming summer tour.

LEFT At the 2021 BRIT Awards in London, Harry brings psychedelic vibes in a '70s square-patterned suit with large lapels and flared trousers. He accentuates the Gucci suit with a brown purse with a bamboo top handle from the Gucci handbag campaign he appears in. During the ceremony, Harry's "Watermelon Sugar" earns him the award for best British single.

LEFT Harry channels music legends like David Bowie and Prince with a boa that accents his custom all-black Gucci leather outfit at the 63rd Annual Grammy Awards in Los Angeles on March 14, 2021. He earned three nominations: best music video for "Adore You," best pop vocal album for *Fine Line*, and best pop solo performance for "Watermelon Sugar," which wins Harry his first Grammy.

RIGHT Harry starts his night at the 63rd Annual Grammy Awards in March 2021 with feathery fun in a lavender boa over a yellow tartan Gucci blazer. The internet likens the checked jacket to the one Alicia Silverstone's character Cher wears in the 1995 movie *Clueless*—and the actress loves it. "Cher would be so honored (and totally approve!!) of this chic look," Alicia writes on Instagram.

Harry never shies away from gender-fluid getups, so for his Harryween Fancy Dress Party concert at Madison Square Garden on October 30, 2021, he dresses up as Dorothy from *The Wizard of Oz*—complete with stockings, custom Gucci ruby red slippers designed by Alessandro Michele, and a stuffed animal Toto sitting in a wicker basket. During his performance he covers "Over the Rainbow." He encourages fans to come in costume too, and they happily oblige. Concertgoers arrive as everything from Oompa Loompas and cowgirl brides to flappers and *Mamma Mia* characters.

Just clowning around at the second night of his Harryween Fancy Dress Party show in October 2021, Harry takes the stage in a white Pierrot clown suit by Gucci, adorned with ruffles and lace fabric with black moon and star appliqués. Harry's band complements his costume, dressing as terrifying clowns. "Please feel free to be whoever it is you've always wanted to be in this room tonight," Harry tells the crowd.

When the Coachella Valley Music and Arts Festival returns in April 2022 following a two-year hiatus, Harry delivers a spectacle that relaunches the event in proper style. In a custom multicolored mirror-detail Gucci jumpsuit that he pairs with a feathery coat, he performs "As It Was" live for the first time. Harry also brings out Shania Twain to duet. He introduces her by saying, "In the car with my mother as a child, this lady taught me to sing."

During the second weekend at Coachella in April 2022, Harry wraps himself in a bright pink, custom Gucci feather coat and completes the outfit with silver boots. He brings out Lizzo—in an orange version of the getup—to sing Gloria Gaynor's "I Will Survive" and 1D's "What Makes You Beautiful." When Harry takes off the coat, he reveals a vest embellished with two large strawberries.

ABOVE Harry sports a custom Gucci ringer tee at *The Howard Stern Show* in May 2022 with bandmates (from left) Mitch Rowland, Sarah Jones, Jonathan Geyevu, Pauli Lovejoy, Elin Sandberg, and Ny Oh. Harry pairs the casual strawberry-patterned top with neon green pants and a chunky beaded necklace from his favorite jewelry brand, Éliou.

RIGHT Harry chooses a casual cool S.S. Daley duck cardigan for his *Harry's House* Spotify launch party on May 19, 2022, the day before his third album drops. Designer Steven Stokey-Daley wrote on Instagram that "this Hazelnut & Tanzy yellow colorway was specifically for Harry by personal request."

ABOVE On the red carpet in September 2022 for the Venice Film Festival premiere of *Don't Worry Darling*, Harry wears a custom double-breasted navy suit and powder-blue shirt with oversize lapels from his HA HA HA collaboration with Gucci creative director Alessandro Michele. He completes the couture ensemble with stacked silver rings, oversize amber-hued sunglasses, and a light-blue manicure.

RIGHT On September 5, 2022, Harry attends the photo-call for *Don't Worry Darling* at the 79th Venice International Film Festival wearing a cream pinstripe jacket, a blue and cream silk scarf, and navy blue wide-leg trousers, all from his HA HA HA collection.

Harry ditches a shirt and goes for an emerald green double-breasted Gucci suit for the premiere of his movie *My Policeman* at the Toronto International Film Festival on September 11, 2022. A matching oversize satin floral brooch, the Gucci Bamboo 1947 top-handle bag—which the brand describes as "a renewal of the masculine world"—and cream heeled boots finalize the look. During the festival, Harry picked up his first acting award when the *My Policeman* cast won the TIFF Tribute Award for Performance.

RIGHT After years of collaborating with Gucci on numerous campaigns, Harry of course wears the Italian designer when *Don't Worry Darling*, the first movie in which he holds a lead role, premieres in New York City on September 19, 2022. The jacket's off-center buttons add a sense of whimsy to the monochromatic 'fit, which Harry finishes with a pink manicure and a ring on almost every finger.

LEFT Harry arrives at the 2023 Grammys sporting a crystal-studded rainbow patchwork Egonlab jumpsuit. The square neckline puts Harry's chest tattoos on full display, and the getup's flared pants sit atop a pair of white heeled boots. The garment boasts 250,000 Swarovski crystals in nine different shades and took more than 150 hours to create. Egonlab's Florentin Glémarec tells *British GQ* that "the color scheme in this creation represents Harry's dynamic personality, his fearless self-expression, and his unwavering commitment to individuality."

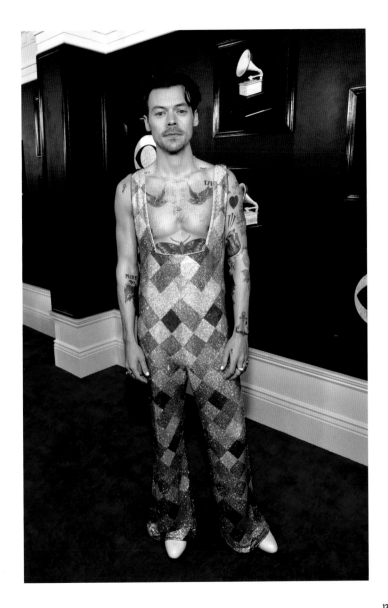

Onstage at the Grammys, Harry electrifies the Crypto.com Arena with a performance of "As It Was" in a long-sleeve, silver fringe Gucci jumpsuit and gold Adidas x Gucci Gazelle sneakers. He looks like a disco ball as he twirls about the stage, not letting a technical issue (the turntable he and his dancers were standing on turned the wrong way!) take away an ounce of energy from the set.

Harry blossoms on the red carpet at the 2023 BRIT Awards on February 11, 2023, pairing his structured custom Nina Ricci by Harris Reed suit with a satin organza flower neckpiece bigger than his head. While the choker dominates the look, Harry adds on his favorite cross necklace and a Gucci banana pendant. Myriad rings, including a Sophie Jane Jewels pearl, an antique Georgian octagonal micro-mosaic ring, and his beloved Gucci lion head, adorn his fingers, as does a manicure with polish from his Pleasing line.

Backed by a six-piece band, Harry opens the 2023 BRIT Awards at O2 Arena in London with a performance of his nominated single "As It Was." The cropped red jacket and high-waisted pants from Gucci make up Harry's first outfit change of the ceremony. After the performance, he dons a sage shirt and deep green suit for the rest of the event. One month after the award show performance, Harry starts the Asia leg of Love on Tour with a performance in Rajamangala National Stadium in Bangkok. Harry also stops in Manila, Singapore, Seoul, and Tokyo and continues to tour through Europe during the 2023 summer.

HEARST HOME

Captions by **Dana Rose Falcone**
Cover and book design by **Jessi Blackham**
Cover photography **Nikki Marie Cardiello**
Back Cover photography **Kevin Mazur/Getty
Images for HS**

Library of Congress Cataloging-in-
Publication Data Available on request

10 9 8 7 6 5 4 3 2 1

Published by Hearst Home, an imprint of
Hearst Books/Hearst Magazine Media, Inc.
300 W 57th Street
New York, NY 10019

Hearst Home, the Hearst Home logo, and
Hearst Books are registered trademarks of
Hearst Communications, Inc.

For information about custom
editions, special sales, premium and
corporate purchases:
hearst.com/magazines/hearst-books

Printed in China
ISBN 978-1-958395-29-5

PHOTO CREDITS:

Neilson Barnard/Getty Images for The Recording Academy 2 Kevin Mazur/
Getty Images for ABA 4–5, 6–7, 126, 127 Jamie McCarthy/Getty Images For
The Rock and Roll Hall of Fame 13 Kevin Mazur/Getty Images for HS 14–15,
38–39, 122, 123, 128–129 Michael Buckner/Variety via Getty Images 19 Christie
Goodwin/Redferns 20–21 Kevin Mazur/Getty Images for TDF Productions
22 Terence Patrick/CBS via Getty Images 24–25, 28, 31, 46 Will Heath/
NBCU Photo Bank/NBCUniversal via Getty Images via Getty Images 26–27
Steve Jennings/Getty Images for Sony Music 29 Jeff Kravitz/FilmMagic for
Sony Music 32–33 Theo Wargo/Getty Images for Victoria's Secret 34 Kevin
Mazur/Getty Images for Sony Music 35 James D. Morgan/WireImage 36
Zak Kaczmarek/Getty Images for ARIA 37 (left) Scott Barbour/Getty Images
for ARIA 37 (right) Rich Fury/Getty Images for Spotify 40 Kevin Mazur/
Getty Images for Pandora 47 Kevin Winter/Getty Images for The Recording
Academy 52, 54, 55 Anthony Pham/via Getty Images 58–59 Joseph Okpako/
WireImage 63 Gilbert Carrasquillo/GC Images 64, 68–69 Nathan Congleton/
NBC via Getty Images 65, 66 James Devaney/GC Images 67 CBS via Getty
Images 71 Matt Crossick/Global/Shutterstock 72 David Fisher/Global/
Shutterstock 73 Nikki Marie Cardiello 76, 77, 78, 79, 144 JC Olivera/WireImage
80 JMEnternational/Getty Images 81, 140 Isabel Infantes/PA Images via
Getty Images 82–83, 92–93 Don Arnold/WireImage 88–89 David M. Benett/
Getty Images for Burberry 90 C Flanigan/Getty Images 91 Nathan Congleton/
NBCU Photo Bank/NBCUniversal via Getty Images 94–95 John Lamparski/
WireImage 95 (left) Mike Coppola/Getty Images 95 (right) J. Lee/FilmMagic
96 Jamie McCarthy/Getty Images 97 Rich Fury/Getty Images for iHeartMedia
98 (left) Kevin Mazur/Getty Images for iHeartMedia 98 (right) Ethan Miller/
WireImage 99 (left) Rich Fury/Getty Images for iHeartMedia 99 (right) Neil
Mockford/GC Images 100 Emma McIntyre/Getty Images for SiriusXM 101
Kevin Mazur/Getty Images for Casamigos 102 Robert Kamau/GC Images
103 Dimitrios Kambouris/Getty Images for The Met Museum/Vogue 104
Matt Winkelmeyer/MG19/Getty Images for The Met Museum/Vogue 105 Will
Heath/NBC/NBCU Photo Bank via Getty Images 106, 107 Terence Patrick/
CBS via Getty Images 109 Kevin Mazur/Getty Images for SiriusXM 110 (left)
Neil Mockford/GC Images 110 (right) Gareth Cattermole/Getty Images 111
(left) Dia Dipasupil/Getty Images 111 (right) Dave J Hogan/Getty Images 112,
141 Richard Young/Shutterstock 114, 115 Nathan Congleton/NBC/NBCU Photo
Bank via Getty Images 116–117 JMEnternational/JMEnternational for BRIT
Awards/Getty Image 118 Anthony Pham via Getty Images 120 Kevin Mazur/
Getty Images for The Recording Academy 121, 138 Theo Wargo/Getty Images
for HS 124–125 Cindy Ord/Getty Images for SiriusXM 130 Kevin Mazur/Getty
Images for Spotify 131 Ernesto Ruscio/Getty Images 132 (left) John Phillips/
Getty Images 132 (right) Daniele Venturelli/WireImage 133 Amy Sussman/
Getty Images 134 Evan Agostini/Invision/AP/Shutterstock 135 Kevin Mazur/
WireImage 136 Stewart Cook/CBS via Getty Images 137 Timothy Norris/
FilmMagic 139 David M. Benett/Max Cisotti/Dave Benett/Getty Images 142
Samir Hussein/WireImage 143 Getty Images- butterfly illustration throughout